Glimpses of
GRACE

2006-7 NMI
MISSION EDUCATION RESOURCES

✳ ✳ ✳

BOOKS

EIGHT STEPS FROM THE EDGE OF HELL
From Addiction to Ministry in Ukraine
by Sherry Pinson

EVERY FULL-MOON NIGHT
Life Lessons from Missionary Kids
by Dean Nelson

GLIMPSES OF GRACE
Mission Stories from Bolivia
by Randy Bynum

THE POWER OF ONE
Compassion as a Lifestyle
by Ellen Decker

SHOULD I KISS OR SHAKE HANDS?
Surviving in Another Culture
by Pat Stockett Johnston

SHOUTS AT SUNRISE
The Abduction and Rescue of Don Cox
by Keith Schwanz

✳ ✳ ✳

ADULT MISSION EDUCATION RESOURCE BOOK

MISSION FAMILIES
Editors: Wes Eby and Rosanne Bolerjack

Glimpses of GRACE

Mission
Stories
from
Bolivia

RANDY BYNUM

Nazarene Publishing House
Kansas City, Missouri

Copyright 2006
by Nazarene Publishing House

ISBN 082-412-2340

Printed in the United States of America

Editor: Wes Eby
Cover Design: Darlene Filley

10   9   8   7   6   5   4   3   2   1

Contents

Randy Bynum and his wife, Kathy, were global missionaries for the Church of the Nazarene for 15 years. They served in Bolivia from 1984-95 and in the Dominican Republic from 1995-99. Primary responsibilities on the field included pastoral education and leadership development.

Randy received a bachelor's degree from Northwest Nazarene University (NNU) in 1974 and a master's degree from Nazarene Theological Seminary, Kansas City, in 1978. He is currently pursuing a doctorate in biblical interpretation through Nazarene Theological College in Manchester, England.

Randy, an ordained elder, was a pastor in Topeka, Kansas, and Berkeley, California, prior to mission service. He is now the pastor of a Spanish-speaking congregation within Lakeview Church of the Nazarene in Nampa, Idaho. He is also director of the online Spanish Course of Study for ministers cosponsored by NNU and Hispanic Ministries for U.S.A./Canada.

Acknowledgments

I would like to acknowledge some of the most wonderful people in the world:

- My wife, Kathy, and our children, Angela, Aaron, and Arlen, who shared these experiences with me
- My mother, Mary Margaret, who continually encouraged me to write
- All the Nazarenes in Bolivia

Que Dios les bendiga ricamente. (May God richly bless them.)

Prologue

Many a volume could be written about our family's mission experiences in Bolivia, but time fails me to tell them all. In these few pages, I would like to give the reader (and listener) just a few glimpses of God's gracious hand at work in the lives of pastors, laypersons, the unsaved, and, yes, even missionaries.

"From his fullness we have **all** received, grace upon grace" (John 1:16, NRSV, emphasis added).

BOLIVIA

PERU

Lake Titacaca

Huarina

La Paz

ANDES MOUNTAINS

Altiplano

CHILE

Potosí

Santa Ana

Santa Cruz

Lomas de Arena

Plan Tres Mil

27 de Mayo

Paurito

BRAZIL

PARAGUAY

ARGENTINA

| 0 | 100 | 200 | 300 km |
| 0 | 100 | | 200 mi |

1
27 de Mayo

The village of 27 de Mayo was hardly more than a wide spot in the road, and the road itself was narrow. In fact, there was little more than two ruts running down through the sandy cane fields of the Santa Cruz countryside. But here in this little pueblo, a group of believers formed the beginning of a Nazarene church.

Melancholy feelings linger whenever I think of our first trip to this village. On that particular day, Mission Director Al Swain and I waited patiently on the street corner for the once-a-day microbus to come. Meanwhile, passing taxi drivers honked repeatedly and signaled to us with their characteristic flip of the hand that said, "I'll take you!" We ignored their calls and continued to wait. Soon we were climbing aboard the short bus, vying with gunny sacks full of flour and other provisions, portable propane tanks, and far too many passengers for a place to sit down. When the paved streets of the city limits gave way to potholed dirt roads of the country, we jostled and jerked our way toward the outlying villages.

From the bus window, a panoramic view of Bolivian rural life presented itself. There were tall stalks

Hauling plantains to market

of greenish-purple sugarcane, rows of yellow corn tops and silk tassels swaying in the breeze, and the unmistakable leaves of the yucca plant, between pastures dotted with cattle, goats, and sheep.

"Este es el camino" (This is the road), the driver signaled to us at last as he slowed to a stop. "You can get off here." You had to have one guiding you who knew the way, for there were no signs signaling the road to 27 de Mayo.

The quiet beauty of the countryside engulfed us as we stepped onto the sandy road. The bustle of the city had been drowned out by tranquil serenity. Our rhythmic footsteps provided background for our conversation as we strode the final leg of the journey.

A grove of trees, a grassy soccer field, and scattered houses made of sticks, mud, and *motacú* (palm) roofs announced that we had arrived in 27 de Mayo. We made our way down the lane to the house of a Nazarene family and were quickly invited inside. However, smiles and warm greetings were soon replaced by wrinkled brows and sad looks. We were ushered to the bedside of a young man who had been studying for the ministry in our theological education extension program. There he lay terribly ill, fighting for his life against tuberculosis. The dreaded disease was in its final stages of attacking his respiratory system, and he appeared to be beyond remedy.

We chatted a bit with the young man and his family, learning the details of his situation. As we sat by his bed, his shallow, rapid, belabored breathing clearly carried the sad message. No doctor needed to inform us that the inevitable was near unless a miracle happened.

Now miracles do happen, and we believe in God's healing touch. It is also true that even the sick ones to whom Jesus reached out and healed with His own hands are no longer with us.

The family asked for prayer, and Al suggested that the new missionary pray. As we bowed our heads, a deep, rare sadness gripped me. Aside from my new-missionary much-less-than-perfect Spanish, I was so moved with emotion that I could hardly choke out a word. Somehow I stammered out a few prayerful sentences, while my heart ached for this young man who had only a few hours or, at most, a few days to live.

The Lord in His wisdom did not choose to touch him in a miraculous way, and the next time we visited the village the young man's bed was empty. A new wooden marker was standing in the family cemetery. While that may remain unexplainable, all the same we have no reason to stop trusting in a loving, living Savior.

In the painful suffering in his eyes, his grasping at the last straws of life, there was a glimpse of our Lord's grace.

In reflecting on that bedside moment, there was a profound and unforgettable sense of God's presence. It would be hard to imagine a person in the Lord's service that was less well-known than this young man. Here he was, lying on a handwoven bed in a dark, thatched-roof house in a jungle village of eastern Bolivia. But well-known is not so terribly important in the Lord's eyes. In the drops of perspiration on his face, the painful suffering in his eyes, his grasping at the last straws of life, there was a glimpse of our Lord's grace.

Paul's prayer for the Philippians reads: "That I may know Him and the power of His resurrection and the **fellowship of His sufferings,** being conformed to His death; in order that I may attain to the resurrection from the dead" (Phil. 3:10-11, NASB, emphasis added).

Yes, that old enemy Death was stalking 27 de Mayo that day. But he did not go unchallenged! Grace and victory were there as well to rob him of his sting. The light of the gospel had already begun to penetrate the spiritual darkness of that Bolivian village. This young man had become a believer along with many others. Not only that, he had been called to the ministry, had said yes to the Lord's call on his life, and to his dying day was living in wholehearted obedience to the leading of the Holy Spirit. He was experiencing that which the world cannot fathom: the "fellowship of Christ's sufferings." In his final gasps of breath in a bittersweet Christian death, he ministered to us by offering a fresh vision of our dying Lord.

27 De Mayo Revisited

Gregorio reached up and pulled a rusty piece of iron out of the crook of the tree and began to bang on the old brake drum dangling from the limb. Its steady clang, clang, clang chimed throughout the village, announcing to everyone that it was time for church service. No automobile factory worker could have ever imagined that the drum he bolted onto a truck so many years before would spend its final years calling villagers to church.

This was no ordinary occasion. This ringing call was an invitation to a dedication service in the new church building for 27 de Mayo. No longer would they have to meet outdoors in the shade of a tree; no longer would they have to suspend the service if the rains came. Now staunch poles from deep within the jungle had been cut and peeled and positioned in the ground. Solid homemade trusses from jungle hardwood had been pounded together with large nails and placed atop the poles. Now fastened firmly on those trusses were shining sheets of zinc-covered metal roofing. Perhaps this wasn't an ornate cathedral, but it was certainly glorious for the Church of the Nazarene in 27 de Mayo.

For a long time their needs called for a building. Not just a place to hold their services out of the blustery rains and the chilling southerly winds, but a structure to clearly identify them in the community.

Pray we did. But as the old adage goes, we also "put feet to our prayers."

But what do you do when you have no building fund savings account, no loan sources to tap, and no wealthy, tithing families? Well, you start by fighting the battle in prayer in the power of God's Spirit and putting unshakable confidence in the Lord for His provision. Then you simply begin to take steps to move ahead with the resources the Lord has given, even if that means little more than the strength of your hands.

Pray we did. But as the old adage goes, we also "put feet to our prayers" and placed the need before the district advisory board. They had some useful ideas of how to proceed and helped us develop some plans. First, we gathered a group of pastors from around the district that knew something about Bolivian-style building. Next, we tapped into a small district building fund that allowed us to buy some nails and sheets of metal roofing. Then one blazing, sultry day, we set out to build 27 de Mayo's building project: a tin roof on poles. It would be a proper beginning, we thought, and perhaps they could add walls, doors, and windows in the future.

Emotions were high the day we began the project. The children scampered enthusiastically to greet us as we drove into the village. "¡Llegó el misionero!

¡Llegó el misionero!" (The missionary has arrived!), they cried out excitedly. In a matter of minutes, we were being jostled by church and village folks crowding around us, who intently soaked up every word as we chatted about the logistics of our plans.

The first step was to travel several kilometers deeper into the jungle where we would find the right kind of trees to make support poles. The villagers knew exactly where to go to find the wood that would provide sturdy poles that would not soon rot. Off we roared with as many strong young men as our '79 Bronco would hold.

What little civilization was out that direction soon faded completely into the rearview mirror, leaving us alone on a narrow trail in thick growth. Did I say "alone"? A huge snake slithered across the road to welcome us, and jungle birds screeched out their warnings of our arrival. When we got out of the vehicle to look for the poles, a strange hum suddenly became apparent. Most people have heard a single mosquito buzzing near their ear. But if you have never heard the audible sound of collective millions of mosquitoes resonating in the jungle, then you have missed a "terrific" experience. I fought off the tiny "vultures," all the while fighting off the thoughts of jungle diseases, while the young men cut the poles and dragged them to the vehicle.

Tree after tree was cut, the limbs stripped, and the heavy poles pushed into the back of the Bronco. When the count was sufficient and nearly enough to snap the Bronco's sagging springs, we climbed in. Sweaty, mosquito-bitten, but happy in the Lord over

Poles for the new church

our new project, we headed back to 27 de Mayo. When that pile of freshly-cut poles was stacked on the site of the future Church of the Nazarene for 27 de Mayo, the scorching sun had disappeared over the horizon, night was upon us, and the day's work was done.

In the light of the next workday, we stretched out measuring lines on the lot, and dirt began to fly as we dug holes. One by one the poles stood strong and steadfast. Two of our youngest and hardiest team members scampered up the poles and nailed the roof structure together as the pieces were handed to them. Finally came the metal sheets, and before the day was over, there stood a solid tin roof on poles that proudly proclaimed: "Here is the Church of the Nazarene."

As the sun slipped behind the horizon and the shadows began to lengthen, the clangs of the brake drum ceased. The folks gathered and quickly filled

New church at 27 de Mayo

up the wooden benches. Gregorio brought a home-made lantern to give light—an empty brake-fluid can filled with kerosene with a wick poked through a hole in the lid. He lit the wick, called the service to order, and prayed an opening prayer. With a well-worn *Gracia y Devoción (Grace and Devotion)* hymnal in hand, he raised his voice and began to sing. All joined in, and hymns began to ring through the night. The Lord's presence and grace flooded the new sanctuary. The light of the gospel was shining in 27 de Mayo, and the jungle's deepest darkness could not put it out.

2
Pastor Manuel

Plan Tres Mil never ceased to fascinate me. Here, barefoot children ran and hollered and played. Their laughter was undiminished by their poverty. Their toys were the simplest of the simple: a stick, a little wheel off a broken toy from a Christmas past, a small plastic truck pulled along by a string, even a pile of tiny rocks. Here, ladies and girls walked to the nearby public water spigot, carrying empty lard cans. They waited their turn in line, then returned with the heavy cans of water balanced on their heads.

Here, pitiful, mangy dogs searched for a spot of shade in which to lie down, twitching and "scritching" in vain to ward off the endless swarms of gnats that pestered them. Music blared from far too many neighborhood bars, accompanied by bottled beer or homemade *chicha* (corn liquor). Plan Tres Mil—here lived the poorest of Bolivia's poor.

It was a section of land in the city of Santa Cruz. This area measured 3,000 hectares (a hectare is 100 by 100 meters, about 2.5 acres), hence the name that means "Plan 3000." A major flood some years before had decimated the dwelling places of many families who lived in makeshift housing along the River Piraí. The government responded by set-

Girls going for water

ting apart this large plot of land. Those who had lost their homes were given first opportunity to buy lots at minimal prices, some as low as U.S. $20. Here the poor folks rebuilt their homes on safer ground.

It was here as well that I had the first meaningful encounter with Pastor Manuel. I had seen him before but did not know him well. This particular afternoon we met one another on the sandy street outside the Plan Tres Mil Iglesia del Nazareno. The relentless tropical sun beat down upon us, drawing beads of sweat from our faces as we stood and conversed.

Bits of interesting information came to light about Manuel and his ministry. He once had pastored on the district, and through a series of unfortunate happenings was no longer able to continue. Sporadic farm work kept the family fed. Regular treatments from the Red Cross center kept his chronic condition of tuberculosis at bay.

In the bond that I sensed developing between colleagues in the ministry, I felt prompted to ask him a key question, "Do you still feel called to the ministry?"

A barely perceptible smile crossed his face as he replied resolutely, "Sí, hermano" (Yes, brother).

"Do you still have the desire to enter active ministry?" Again the answer was affirmative.

"Stay involved in the local church," I counseled him. "Keep close to the Lord in prayer. Come and continue to study in the extension education courses for pastors, and let's pray for an open door for you to do what God has called you to do." A swarthy Bolivian hand reached out and grasped a light-complexioned missionary hand, and a firm shake sealed the deal.

Manuel's gentle, teachable spirit and homespun wisdom compensated for his small amount of formal schooling.

Tuberculosis was not the only factor that was working against Manuel. He was already into midlife and past the age of Bolivian life expectancy, his wife was frail and often ill, and he had five children to support.

In the coming months, Manuel kept his word to begin studying once again. He came regularly to the Monday night extension education courses. Manuel's gentle, teachable spirit and homespun wisdom compensated for his small amount of formal schooling.

We kept praying for an opportunity for ministry. The months passed, turning into years, but we

Pastor Manuel, his wife, Benita, and their daughter

kept believing until one day a door swung open. Manuel and his family moved to a country location and began to plant a little congregation of believers. Fond recollections of that group come to mind.

I remember meeting for a Sunday service in a small room of his home. Upwards of 20 gathered to worship the Lord, and the cement walls echoed with our singing and clapping. When it was time to bring the message of the Word, Manuel introduced me.

"It is a real privilege to have 'Hermanos Randys' with us today," he said in unmistakable country slang. It was no more than a couple of steps from my chair to the small wooden table that served as a pulpit. The audience listened intently as the Word was proclaimed to them.

On another visit, the group asked if there was money in the district budget for a guitar. Up to that time they were singing entirely a cappella. I sadly had to tell them the truth: "There's no money, hermanos." I challenged them to price the guitar they wanted, raise the money, even a few Bolivianos at a time, and work toward their goal of buying that guitar. I knew this could have been a project of months or years, if it ever happened at all. How wrong I was!

When I visited again in a few weeks, they had sacrificed and pooled their pesos to reach their goal. All smiles, they proudly displayed the shiny new guitar they had purchased from an instrument dealer in the market. I was to be one of the first to play it for their service. What an honor to do so!

I recall a baptismal service in the small cement stock tank behind their house. The tank was not large, and the water was not exactly sparkling clean, but then neither was the Jordan River. The weather had turned cool as well, with a southern wind chilling the day. How often it seemed that such a bitter wind came just in time for our baptismal services. The presence and grace of the Lord and the testimonies of new believers, however, took the edge off the cold.

On one occasion they invited me to stay for lunch. I can still see Benita, Manuel's wife, pulling strips of dried beef off the clothesline. The hot sun had turned the meat to jerky, preserving it in the absence of refrigeration.

There were times of difficulty; for example, the day Manuel's meager salary was stolen by someone he thought was a trusted friend. Then came the unspeakable tragedy of their youngest son catching his toe in a bike chain. He received nothing more than home remedies for the injury. Unbeknown to them, the boy was developing gangrene, and by the time the realization hit and they urgently transported him to the nearest clinic, the hour of healing opportunity had passed. The infection's poison had advanced its sinister grip; hope was gone. What could have been treated so easily became fatal.

If ever a pastor demonstrated the grace of God under pressure, it was Manuel.

If ever a pastor demonstrated the grace of God under pressure, it was Manuel. If ever a person reflected Jesus' attributes of a "man of sorrows and acquainted with grief," it was this humble man. Living in abject poverty, working manual farm labor at minimum Bolivian wage (nowhere near U.S. minimum wage standards), suffering the lingering effects of tuberculosis, having a large family to feed, caring for a frail wife in poor health, losing a beloved youngest son, he continued faithful to the Lord and strong in ministry. Never was there a more encouraging example of sacrifice!

Manuel lived out what Paul proclaimed to the Corinthians: "Therefore we do not lose heart. Though outwardly we are wasting away, yet inwardly we are being renewed day by day. For our light and momentary troubles are achieving for us an eternal glory that far outweighs them all" (2 Cor. 4:16-17). Manuel may be one of the first in line for that glory.

3
The Philosophy Course

The lofty Andes mountains towered in the distance as the district superintendent and I drove along the two-lane highway from La Paz to Huarina. The dazzling snow-covered peaks offered the utmost in mountain majesty. Their brilliant white purity seemed to stretch from the already high elevation of the plain to the very edges of heaven itself.

Along the road little adobe houses speckled the plain, seemingly miniature in comparison to the mountains. Dark weaving lines of piled rock made fences to divide fields or corral animals. Aymara folks, young and old alike, hoed the fields and tended their llamas and alpacas.

Soon the rays of bright afternoon sun glistened off the still waters of Lake Titicaca. With that signal we knew we were arriving at our destination. I had left the steamy, humid lowlands of Santa Cruz to spend a few days teaching an *intensivo* (intensive training course) to our pastors in the arid, clear coolness of the altiplano.

When we pulled off the pavement onto the dirt street, the local pastor of Huarina welcomed us with

On the road to Huarina

a warm smile. He grabbed one of my bags at once, and after a quick greeting we walked a little ways down the street to the local hotel.

Travelers on their own would have to search for this place. No flashing neon sign announced its location, nor indicated vacancy or no vacancy. My guess is that a full house was a rare occurrence. Only a small handwritten sign on the outside adobe wall told us we had come to the right place.

We opened the solid metal gate with a creak and stepped into the waiting room. The pastor called out to announce our arrival. We waited in the stillness until a young man appeared and attended to us. After introductions and my ID noted on a tablet, we walked across the interior courtyard. The "innkeeper" proudly showed me to my room.

With no tape measure in hand, I estimated the room to be about the size of my office, maybe 9' x 12'. A small table and a single bed furnished the room. The swaybacked metal frame of the bed was not one a chiropractor would recommend. A llama-wool blanket, accompanied by two other wool blankets folded neatly at the end, covered a bottom sheet. The table had a lamp and a washbasin.

I set my bags down, and the young man took me across the courtyard to explain the single bathroom shared by all guests. There was no door on the outside, but fortunately there was a plastic curtain. Inside, a concrete wall separated two divisions. On the left was the you-know-what, and on the right was a shower that appeared to have functioned some time in the distant past. A rusty chunk of galvanized pipe jutted from the wall. At the end of it, an electric showerhead hung with dangling wires that gave little hope of ever operating again.

On the left was the you-know-what, and on the right was a shower that appeared to have functioned some time in the distant past.

The hotel man apologized for the lack of running water, but added encouragingly that he would go every morning early and dip two buckets of water from the lake for the guests. To wash up, I could fill the washbasin from the bucket and take it back to my room. Since neither the room nor the water was heated, and frost was on the ground every morning, it was immediately apparent that Jesus' advice to Judas would come in handy here, "What you are about to do, do quickly" (John 13:27b).

I remember wondering that first evening if I was really going to need all three wool blankets.

How naive I was about altiplano winter nights! My doubts were soon dispelled. Upon retiring for the night, I pulled one wool blanket over me, then another. Before long, the third one. About a half hour later I got up, put on my jogging suit, and crawled back into bed. Another 20 minutes passed. I arose again and added an altiplano stocking hat to my colorful outfit and huddled back beneath the heavy pile of wool blankets. Not exactly toasty warm, but warm enough, I finally drifted off to sleep.

I arose again and added an altiplano stocking hat to my colorful outfit and huddled back beneath the heavy pile of wool blankets.

As the morning sun peered over the mountains to see what we were up to, the pastors met at the Huarina church to hold the first class. The wooden floors squeaked out their welcome to us as we made our way to the front of the sanctuary. A rectangular wooden table that would serve as my lectern received my pile of notes without comment. A homemade chalkboard stood shyly to one side, offering its services as the only teaching aid.

We began the class session on *hora Boliviana* (Bolivian time), that is, when several students finally arrived. They continued to come until by midmorning there was a good-sized class.

The only philosophy textbook available in Spanish was a work translated from English. It was essentially a rendition of Bostonian personalism. None of my students had ever heard of either Boston or personalism. Its author, I'm confident, had little anticipation of ever having a hearing among South American pastors.

While I found Bolivian students to be intelligent, not many of them had extensive academic training. I did my best to present some basic philosophical concepts. Though the text seemed as though it were written long ago in another galaxy far, far away, nonetheless, we made some progress.

About midmorning throughout the course, welcomed rays of sunlight would shine their way through the sanctuary windows for a while and warm things up a bit. I was dressed in two or three layers of clothes to keep the cold out, and these were the few fleeting moments of each day that I actually felt warm. Perhaps a few inspiring rays of insight warmed our minds as well.

Lunchtime was a highlight of the day for all. In addition to giving a break from the studies, it offered time to enjoy delicious altiplano cuisine. One meal stands out in particular: a huge plate piled high with large, fried noodles was set in front of me, topped with two slices of tangy fried cheese. To wash it down, there was steaming, sweet tea. Since I was the guest of honor, they served me first and gave me the largest portion, then watched to see if I would eat it all.

On the last day of the course just before the final exam, one of the pastors came up to my desk with a worried look. When he asked to talk a minute, I could see the concern in his eyes over the test that was before him. He was tall and somewhat gangly. He had dressed his best for this occasion in a well-worn suit that was out of style. Its size, about

Altiplano
ministerial
students

38 medium, squeezed a pastor who was 42 long. There was little doubt that it was the only suit he owned.

He began by expressing his worry over being able to pass the course. I tried to encourage him; perhaps he had done better than he thought, I suggested. Then he explained his difficulty: "My father never taught me to read," he said sadly. In that single sentence he had spoken volumes. His father was evidently able to read but had not taken the time to teach his son. Or perhaps his father had plenty of money to send his son to school but took no interest in doing so. It was doubtful that the pastor had been able to attend more than a couple of years of grammar school, if at all. Yet he had learned to read somehow and was now in the course of study for ministers. Even further, he was capturing at least some basic ideas in the introduction to philosophy. I moved to his side and grasped his arm. "Do your best," I encouraged him, and we proceeded with the exam. Although some got through by the proverbial skin of their teeth, he and all the others did pass the course.

With the exam done and the course finished, I packed, left the "Huarina Grand Hotel" (not its real name), and climbed once again into the district superintendent's Toyota jeep. With a warm Bolivian-style "hasta luego" (good-bye), I left Huarina. The transmission whined, and the tires hummed on the pavement once again as the waters of Lake Titicaca shimmered in the background.

How well I had taught philosophy was debatable. It was also an open question who had learned more and grown more, the students or the professor. Some things left no room for doubt, however. Not only in the class, but over meals and at break times, these pastors and I had shared with one another many interesting experiences along with valuable insights into life and ministry. We had grown together in Christian fellowship and brotherhood, and my appreciation for altiplano pastors had deepened. The Lord had taken what He values more than anything in the universe: people, His own creation. In this case it was Aymara young men drawn together from the area around Lake Titicaca. By His grace, He had chosen them for ministry. Now He had set them on the road of discipleship, and they were doing their best to prepare and follow Him. Certainly He had ordained their ministries for evangelizing that great altiplano high plain with the message of Christian holiness. And God allowed me to see His grace one more time.

4
The Grace-full Reception

When Abraham received the heavenly visitors and prepared a feast for them from the best that he had,* he had nothing on Pastor Ignacio. Whenever we went to visit him and his little country church, he always bounded out to meet us with genuine joy on his face.

On one particular hot and sultry Tuesday afternoon, I dropped by his house. With no cell phones, no land lines, no beepers, no E-mail, there was no way to contact him beforehand to let him know I was coming. All the same, Ignacio greeted me with a Bolivian handshake and pat on the shoulder.

"Quick, bring a chair for Hermano Randy," he told his son. A couple of homemade chairs with woven seats appeared a minute later, and he invited me to sit out in the yard.

Although just past noon, a bit of shade under the papaya trees sheltered us. In typical Bolivian fashion, he brought me up-to-date on how he, the family, and the church were doing.

---

*See Genesis 18:1-7.

"Fix us something to eat," he said to his wife, Flora. As "the elders" talked, soft-spoken Flora stoked up the fire. She and her daughters scurried around, and before the hour was up, out came a huge plate of food.

Since I was the guest, the whole family graced me by standing and watching while I ate first.

Flora brought the large platter over and sat it on a little table between us. We immediately dropped whatever we had been talking about to concentrate on having a bite of lunch. The red-and-white covering cloth came off, and steam rose from the large serving plate half-filled with boiled potatoes, the other half piled with boiled eggs. I had never seen that many eggs and potatoes on one plate on one table at one time. If you had been there and had seen their poverty, you would have been grateful and prayed as I did: "Loving Father, we thank You for this food . . ."

After a long silence, I said to Pastor Ignacio, "Shall we eat?"

"We?" he replied. "No, that's for you!"

Since I was the guest, the whole family graced me by standing and watching while I ate first. It sort of felt like eating dinner by yourself onstage in front of an audience. I did feel honored, of course, but wondered how I could possibly eat that much food. I hoped I could eat enough to convince them that I really did like their food and appreciated their hospitality.

I have never cracked and eaten so many boiled

Pastor Ignacio and his family

eggs or stuffed so many potatoes down myself before or since. I didn't keep count, but I know it was a record. When I was done and they were sure that I had had enough, the rest of them together ate what was left on the plate.

I stayed awhile longer and did my best to fulfill my mission for that day: to listen to and encourage a country pastor. Certainly I was the one more ministered to. The Lord said, "Whoever receives you, receives Me" (Matt. 10:40*a*, NRSV). Never had I been more well-received. As always, Ignacio had treated the Lord and me like royalty.

As they received me, so they received the gospel—in simple country fashion. But potential twists in the reception of the message were myriad. Culture. Customs. Country medicine-men with their mixture of herbs, home remedies, legends, and semi-spiritualistic chants. Along with traditional syncretistic Catholicism, all these threatened to alter the biblical message.

The Lord is well aware, certainly, of the spiritual needs of the human heart, as well as the endless devices of the fleshly mind that resist the fullness of the ministry of the Holy Spirit. The Word, however, was received. The well-worn, black-covered *Santa Biblia* (Holy Bible) was safely guarded, carefully read, regularly proclaimed, and lived out like it is in every culture—seen through a glass darkly, knowing in part, prophesying in part (1 Cor. 13). Yet Ignacio and clan and neighbors in their graciousness received both the Messenger and the message.

5
The Message

The afternoon sun turned much redder and sank lower in the sky than it should have for a journey of this length on foot. But the message had to be delivered, and travel options were few. The single daily bus along that country route had dropped me off in 27 de Mayo some time ago and would not be back again until morning. I had delivered the message to Gregorio, Justa, and the others, and now the rest of the journey would have to be done by the mode of transportation that the Bolivians humorously call "línea dos" (bus line No. 2), that is, two legs. I had to take the message on to the village of Paurito.

Flocks of resplendently green parrots reflected the last rays of sun as they flapped their way toward their evening roost. I expected them to say something to me as they passed; a polite greeting perhaps. But then their simple squawks reminded me that they were country parrots after all and had not had any educational opportunities. Sadly, they were no more articulate than a crow or a magpie.

Their screeches were accompanied by the most vocal of evening frogs, who were already greeting the lengthening shadows with their "peers" and "ny-ers" and "rorts" (I never heard a Bolivian frog that said "ribbet").

With a long, winding, sandy road ahead, it was a perfect opportunity to enjoy the rare delights of the Bolivian countryside. There was an endless variety of greenery—from tall, jungle hardwood trees, to thick underbrush, to cane fields.

The country beauty faded, however, as the miles stretched on. The rosy glow of sunset faded, and complete darkness fell. The nighttime calls of birds and animals began to intensify as they mingled with my thoughts and prayers. Yes, I was concerned about safety, but I never felt any fear. There were things that happened along that road from time to time, it is true. But compared to walking a backstreet in a big city at night, it was quite safe. Besides, the Lord's presence did not leave me all alone.

Sore feet and legs were crying out, "We have had quite enough for one day, thank you very much!"

Walking long distances gives you a much different perspective on life. It even begins to illumine some biblical narratives in a way that aren't readily visible when roaring down the road in an SUV. The road to Jericho seems much more real; the late afternoon conversation with the Lord on the way to Emmaus takes on new dimensions. A foot-washing after such a trip would certainly have been refreshing as well. Bible times do not seem nearly so distant.

The road seemed endless. Some three hours of steady strides later the lights of "metropolitan" Paurito gave a soft glow in the sky ahead. I arrived there just before 8:00 in the evening. As you can easily

Robertina weaving a sombrero

imagine, sore feet and legs were crying out, "We have had quite enough for one day, thank you very much!" Add to that a growling stomach sending unmistakable signals that it was way past dinnertime. I had built up, as Phineas Bresee would say, "a most excellent appetite."*

I headed straight for the Nazarene missionary's bed-and-breakfast, that is, Gabriel and Robertina's house. Their standing invitation assured me that I was always welcome, and this was no exception. At last I stood at their front gate and called out to them to announce my arrival.

The aroma of empanadas, sizzling on the stove, invited me irresistibly. Robertina and one of the chil-

---

*Carl Bangs, *Phineas F. Bresee* (Kansas City: Beacon Hill Press, 1953), 71.

dren greeted me with a smile. She pulled up a chair and told me to sit down at once. The empanadas continued to fry as she brewed some strong coffee to go with them.

Bolivians usually don't ask you how you want your coffee, if you want it black, or with cream or sugar. They just load it with sugar, like everybody is supposed to drink it. Names of diet sweeteners and artificial coffee creamers have never entered their vocabulary.

As the plate of hot onion-filled empanadas and a mug of steaming sweet coffee were set in front of me, I thought about the late hour. That was not my usual evening meal, and I wondered if I would be able to sleep that night. Ordinarily, that would have been enough to keep me awake for hours. But the Word of the Lord is quite clear about these kinds of situations: "Stay in that house, eating and drinking whatever they give you" (Luke 10:7a). I was in no mood to complain. I must admit that never did empanadas and coffee taste any better. Sleep? *Who needs it*, I thought. *I'll deal with tomorrow when tomorrow comes.*

We exchanged greetings and caught up on one another's families, and then they showed me my bed. I lay awake for several minutes . . . well, maybe as many as five or six. Suddenly, it seemed, the roosters were crowing just a few feet away to announce the dawn.

The message I had to deliver to our *hermanos* (Christian brothers and sisters) was about our youth camp planned that year in Paurito. Details had to be

Sunday School class at Paurito

arranged and buildings reserved. It was the first time they had attempted that kind of ministry for the youth.

Some weeks later, the big event came. Directed by our Bolivian pastors and lay leaders, it was quite a success. Enthusiasm was high, and the eyes of the entire pueblo were on the Nazarene young people. Though the setting was certainly rustic, the Santa Cruz youth had plenty of food, fun, and fellowship. There was time for soccer and volleyball. There were devotional times with singing, guitar playing, and biblical messages from our district's best speakers.

Best of all, there were opportunities for newcomers to experience the grace and forgiveness of the Savior and for Christians to deepen their walk with the Lord. The youth camp in Paurito gave a clear message to everyone in the entire village: it is great to know Jesus Christ and won-

Once again, I observed God's grace wrapped up in a simple "message."

derful to follow the Lord. Once again, I observed God's grace wrapped up in a simple "message."

I walked sandy roads to deliver that message. Others walked before us, and the Lord of the harvest will send others to continue the work when we are gone. I'm not sure what you think of your feet; most people don't think of theirs as particularly beautiful. Isaiah said feet are beautiful, if they are taking the message of the Lord to those who need to hear. "How beautiful are the feet of those who bring good news of good things!" (Romans 10:15, NASB, quoting Isaiah 52:7). Walking, riding horseback, taking a bus, flying a mission plane, whatever the means of travel, somehow our feet have to get there with the message.

6
The Other Side
of the Wall

Huge, thick weeds that seemed more like small trees towered over our heads and threatened to discourage us before we had barely begun. Persistent prayer and patient searching had led our footsteps to this new lot in Santa Cruz, which was purchased for our district center, well-located but undeveloped. There was only one thing to do: dig in and start working. We had no state-of-the-art machinery, no power tools, no weed whackers, no heavy mowers. We were driven by the vision of a weed-filled lot transformed into a new district center.

Foreheads beaded with perspiration and muscles strained as a group of strong pastors and laymen attacked the formidable growth. Our only mechanical help was the Nazarene community "back-hoe," that is, back bent and hoe in hand. Soon the overgrown weeds went toppling, and wooden stakes took their place. First steps had been taken, emotions were high and spirits joyful.

Before we could put up a building, however, there was a prerequisite: a security wall to keep out intruders. An open, unfenced yard, like many houses have in the United States, would never do. The constant threat of thievery called for a high brick wall with pieces of broken glass imbedded in the top. The finishing touch was a strong, iron gate at the entrance.

Shovels dug in; dirt flew. Lines were set, and the footing poured. Local bricklayers built the security wall, and, in a matter of days, a Work and Witness team was on their way to begin the construction.

Cliff Shaum brought a team from Michigan to erect our first building—a library and classroom combination for our pastoral training program. They also hoped to begin a district parsonage on the same lot. With a skilled, unbeatable team, which included several professional construction workers, the project advanced rapidly.

The morning the team began, the property was bustling with brisk activity. As enthusiastic calls for "mezcla" (mortar) and "ladrillos" (bricks) rang out, children from the neighborhood crowded around the gate to see what was happening. Curious onlookers stopped to gaze at the new construction. This neighborhood had not seen such activity for years.

On the south side of the lot, a spindly, thorny tree wound its way up beside the wall, blocking the construction of the library. The tree had to be taken out. I pulled on heavy gloves to avoid the thorns and leaned a ladder against the wall. Up I went and began to chop away at the top limbs.

This trip up the ladder was the first time any one of us had ever viewed the other side of the wall. There lay a large lot, empty except for one thing—a makeshift house. Slabs of clapboard and odd pieces

Building
the new
district
center

of tin formed a small dwelling. It sat right up against the wall that separated us.

The house was dwarfed by the huge lot. A young mother was going about her morning duties, stoking a wood fire for cooking, hanging clothes out to dry, and tending to the children scampering here and there. One thing was obvious: they were caretakers of the property. If they had been the owners, they would have had a larger brick house.

My head was already sticking above the wall, and the lady's eyes met mine.

"Buenos días, Señora," I called out. "Do you want this firewood?" I offered.

"No," she responded simply, "that wood just smokes a lot."

"That's fine."

So went the first conversation between two non-talkative neighbors.

The next morning, the woman's husband came to see if there was work. He was a skilled bricklayer, he said. We were a little wary of someone that we didn't know but offered to give him a try.

"What's your name?" I asked.

"Rosendo."

Bits of "Anglicized Spanish" interchanged with "Spanishized English," began to melt the barriers.

I introduced him to the group, and he jumped in and went right to work. He showed quickly that he truly was a skilled craftsman and knew how to lay a straight row of bricks. The guys on the team liked him and his work, and they got along well in spite of their lack of a common language. Bits of "Anglicized Spanish" interchanged with "Spanishized English," along with big helpings of genuine Christian friendliness, began to melt the barriers.

It wasn't long before we had the privilege of meeting the whole family. A couple of team members took the initiative to venture next door to get acquainted. There they discovered a young boy, named Marcos, with extensive bandages along his side and leg. His mother, Gladis, explained that he had been severely burned. With no money for expensive treatment, they did what most Bolivian families do: get along the best they could with home remedies and minimal treatment.

That night at dinner, the fellows on the team began to talk. They could not get the badly burned boy next door out of their minds. They were determined to see that Marcos had the needed treatments. The next morning, they asked Rosendo and

Gladis for permission to take the boy to the clinic. They continued to take him for medical care during the two weeks they were there, and the lad began to mend. Willing and compassionate team members, together with a physician's skillful hands, began to make the difference in this young boy's need.

The blazing hot workdays stretched on; soon the Work and Witness project was drawing to a close. A tremendous amount of progress had been made on the district center. The walls for the library were up; the roof was on. In addition, the new district parsonage had walls up as well. On the last day of work, rafters for the parsonage roof—mahogany, no less!—were set into place.

Rosendo, Gladis, and children came to a banquet before the team left. Friendships had been formed; lives had been touched. The boy with severe burns was now well on his way to wholeness. All of us shed tears and exchanged words of gratitude to the Lord and to one another. After a round of hugs and handshakes for everyone, it was time to go.

After the team left, local laborers finished the parsonage. Soon District Superintendent Macedonio Daza, his wife, Christina, and their children moved into their new district parsonage. They continued the friendship with Rosendo and Gladis and invited them to church. One Sunday they agreed to go, so everyone piled into the minibus and headed for the Barrio Lindo church where Macedonio was pastor.

Tremendous power flows where the gospel is preached clearly and lived out faithfully. The convicting power of the Holy Spirit, together with the love of the Daza family and the Barrio Lindo people, gripped the hearts of Rosendo and his family. Not many Sundays passed before they had given their hearts to the Lord and had become a part of the local Nazarene church fellowship.

Rosendo's testimony of God at work in his life was tremendous. God had given him a new heart and a new life with many positive changes. But there was also a price to pay for becoming a Christian.

> **As Rosendo entered the house where he had always been welcome, an icy silence filled the room.**

Soon after his conversion, he rode the bus across town to visit his parents and family, as was his custom on Sunday afternoon. As Rosendo entered the house where he had always been welcome, the conversation suddenly stopped, and an icy silence filled the room.

"So, you have become an evangelical Christian?" they accused.

"Yes, it's true," he admitted. But before Rosendo could tell them of all the marvelous things the Lord was accomplishing in his life and for his family, they showed him the door and told him never to return. The promise of the Lord for such occasions, however, remained faithful, "And everyone who has left houses or brothers or sisters or father or mother or children or farms for My name's sake, will receive many times as much, and will inherit eternal life" (Matt. 19:29, NASB).

The joy of salvation more than offset the sacrifices. Gladis fairly glowed when she told of the change in Rosendo when he came to know the Lord. In times past, he would get his pay at the end of the week and head straight for the bar with his friends. There amid the raucous laughter, the card games, the jovial slaps on the back, he would drink himself into a stupor and his family into abject poverty. Far into the night without a centavo in hand, he would stumble home with only curses and abuses for his wife and children. Gladis did extra washing and ironing to earn enough to put food on the table.

Then one golden day he arrived home on pay-day with money in hand. Gladis was thoroughly confused, she admitted. *Still so early in the day*, she thought. *Could he be drunk already?* She stared in disbelief, certain that somehow he had mistakenly ended up at the house early. He drew his full pay out of his pocket and handed her the money, leaving her dumbfounded.

"Let's go to the market," he declared with a grin. "We're going to buy food, and if there is any money left, clothes for the kids," he added confidently.

All of these things slowly sank into Gladis's consciousness. Not until they had walked to the bus stop and near the open-air market did the reality hit home. That day, she said, she was walking on air.

Such incredible changes by God's grace would cause anyone to take a few steps on air to think of Rosendo and Gladis. The Lord took a Work and Witness team, an act of compassion for a boy, Christian neighbors Macedonio and Christina, and with the power of His forgiving grace gave new lives to the people on the other side of the wall.

7
The Right Road

No map showed anyone how to get there. You just had to know the way, or have an experienced guide, or remember well the directions given to you —none of which we did. There really wasn't even a road—just the wisp of a winding trail that faded into the landscape like camouflage.

We were on our way to Lomas de Arena, an area of sand dunes outside Santa Cruz. Alongside them lay a crystal pool of glistening water, just perfect for a baptismal service. Pastor Lucio and the congregation from the Villa Pillín, a neighborhood within Santa Cruz, had piled into a truck and gone on ahead. Kathy, the kids, and I had packed a lunch and threw in a big thermos of water. With an extra gas can on the back, we jumped in our Bronco and headed for the country to join them.

We did fine for a while, and the way seemed right. But then there was that one terrible, fateful turn. Perhaps the wise old Hebrew had such an experience in mind when he penned, "There is a way that seems right to a man . . ." (Prov. 14:12).

As we turned and rounded the bend, our trail suddenly became a riverbed. That was not so bad in and of itself; often back roads in Bolivia follow such courses. It soon became apparent, however, that this was not the road we wanted. The clues were all too obvious.

Suddenly, our Bronco began to lurch and jerk. Then it chugged to a stop altogether. I quickly shifted into four-wheel drive. The engine lugged as spinning wheels threw sand behind them in a futile attempt to move forward. We stayed in exactly the same spot and began to sink into quicksand. It was hard to tell which sunk farther and faster—the vehicle or our spirits.

"We're sinking!" I snapped. "Hurry and get out!"

I honestly pictured our vehicle disappearing out of sight. I could hardly stand the image that was flashing through my mind: our beloved Bronco being sucked into the sands of an old riverbed, never to be seen again. But wait! The living nightmare stopped short. It didn't completely happen. When the wheels were out of sight and the sand was at the bottom of the doors, the sinking stopped. Perhaps things would have been much easier if it had just disappeared into the sand. Then our choices would have been much simpler.

But now what? The feeling of total helplessness swept over us all as we stood on the sand and contemplated the whole ordeal. Fortunately, it was a small area of quicksand, and we ourselves were not sinking out of sight as well.

We could join Job and cry and curse the day of our birth.

We considered our options. We could stay there, hope for the best and allow the baptismal to go on without us. We could try to find the right road and wait for the church group as they returned. We could leave the vehicle and go on to the baptismal on foot, but how many more kilometers awaited us in that relentless, blazing, tropical sun? We could yell and scream real loud. We could join Job and cry and curse the day of our birth. None of our options seemed too rosy.

There we stood, scratching our heads and contemplating several possible solutions. Someone observed a farmhouse not too far away. Perhaps they would be nice country folks and lend us a shovel. So we went to ask.

Wrong we were! When we asked the *campesino* (man who lives in the country), his eyes lit up as he said, "Sure, I'll lend you a shovel . . . for 100 Bolivianos!" (about U.S. $25). We didn't have 100 Bolivianos, and we wouldn't have given it to him if we did. What audacity! We were steaming on the inside but managed to keep our composure on the outside as we replied, "No, gracias." Sadly we trudged back to the Bronco and on to "plan B."

We believed we had gone far enough that Lomas de Arena should not be too much farther. Whether wise or unwise, we finally decided that Kathy and kids should stay with the vehicle. I would continue on foot to the baptismal and bring back help as soon as possible.

The sun seemed to have little compassion as the sandy miles stretched ahead. But within an hour, my spirits lifted as the dunes of Lomas de Arena loomed in front of me. When I walked over the last hill and entered the scene, everyone was having a wonderful time—sharing their food, playing in the sand, splashing in the water. Somehow, I wasn't much in the mood for food and fun.

I explained to Pastor Lucio our dilemma. He felt that it would be too much to go and dig out the vehicle, then return for the baptismal service. The candidates were ready. "Let's go ahead with the baptism," he said, "and finish as soon as possible. Then we will help you."

I was not in a position to bargain. My stomach was already knotted over leaving Kathy and the kids for such a long time. But everyone else was more confident than I in the protection of the Lord's guardian angels.

One by one the radiant Christians entered the water. They stood knee-deep and by testimony proclaimed their stories of God's saving grace in their lives. With their hearts they believed, and with their mouths they confessed Jesus Christ as Lord. Then we dipped them into the warm, clear waters in the name of the Father, Son, and Holy Spirit. What an inspiring moment! Caught up in the joy these believers expressed over their new-found faith, I felt as though I, too, had become a Christian all over again.

In closing, we sent several hymns and choruses ringing across the water. Among them was that favorite baptismal confession: "I have decided to follow Jesus . . . no turning back, no turning back." Wide smiles covered the faces of these new saints as they stood in the edge of the water and posed for a final picture.

Pastor Lucio *(left)*, his wife, and baptismal candidates

Meanwhile, what about my family? If thieves wanted to have the Bronco or anything in it, they could dig it out of the sand and have it. It could be replaced, but not my wife and kids. *How are they doing?* I wondered. *Are they OK?* Mental pins and needles relentlessly poked me as I thought about them. I kept taking deep breaths and praying the Lord's protection over them.

The service had only taken about 20 minutes, but it seemed like forever. At last several of the strong young men of the group were by my side, taking long, quick strides back down the sandy road toward the scene of the disaster. The rest of the group stayed at the sand dunes to play and clean up.

What a relief when we arrived back at the scene! Kathy and kids were all fine, but the time had drug by slowly for them as they wondered when we were coming.

With nothing more than our hands and some sticks, we began to dig. Progress was excruciatingly slow in the face of such an enormous task. The self-ish neighbor stood at a distance and observed. Suddenly, by God's providential hand, another vehicle appeared and offered assistance. Kathy hopped aboard with our youngest son, Arlen, and returned to the sand dunes to ask for more help.

Later she returned on foot, carrying Arlen in the blazing afternoon sun. Along with her were Pastor Lucio and, thankfully, more strong hands. Pastor Lucio led the way as he said the most important words of the day, "First thing we need to do is to pray." We bowed our heads. We believed the Lord was there, concerned about our situation and willing to help us.

After prayer we all spread out to look for a post or log or something of the sort. Soon someone happily returned with an eight-foot length of a solid oak tree trunk on his shoulder. Perfect! Things were beginning to look up.

"Got a spare tire?" they asked.

"You bet!"

We laid the tire flat on the sand beside one of the sunken wheels. We stuck the end of the oak log under the edge of the rim and used the spare as a fulcrum.

"Heave ho, guys! ¡Uno, dos, y tres!"

We grunted and groaned and began to rhythmically bounce on the end of the oak post until that one wheel came up a bit. As it slurped out of the wet sand, we held it up with the log while others put branches underneath. Then we let the Bronco back down on a firmer footing.

We went around and did the same to the other

wheels. By this time, we had already spent several hours and the afternoon shadows were signaling sunset. Finally the last wheel was up and sitting above ground. What a fantastic sight!

The vehicle lurched forward. I jammed it into second and floored it again.

I climbed in and started the engine. I feared that the vehicle might move a few feet forward and sink again. To prevent that, we put branches in front of the vehicle to provide a path for the wheels. It was already in four-wheel drive, and I put it in first gear.

"Pray hard!" I called out.

I held my breath and gunned the engine for all it was worth. The vehicle lurched forward. I jammed it into second and floored it again. It lunged ahead toward the bank of the riverbed. Shouts of joy rose heavenward as we reached solid ground.

In a matter of seconds, we were finally back on the *right* road. When the truck with the rest of the group came along, we all headed back home.

Alongside the road, as is common, a *campesino* was hitchhiking into town. Guess who? The same man who wanted to rent us a shovel. What sweet revenge it would have been, I thought, to roar past him and leave him in the dust, or to stop and say, "Oh, you need a ride into town? Sure. 100 Bolivianos." But we didn't. He gave us a sheepish look as we stopped and called out, "Sure, hop in the back."

This baptism was a means of grace for some new Christians and also for some "old" missionaries.

We saw once again that God takes care of His own, and there is no greater place to be than in the Body of Christ. Walking with the Lord is not only the *right* road, it is the *only* road.

As the evening shadows lengthened, Pastor Lucio, newly baptized Christians, mature believers, a missionary family, even a less-than-generous *campesino* all headed back to town together on the right road. "But the path of the righteous is like the light of dawn, that shines brighter and brighter until the full day" (Prov. 4:18, NASB).

8
The Toolbox

"Are you sure you can get me on your moto with a guitar and a suitcase?" I queried in disbelief.

"No problem, Jefe" (Chief), the driver assured me. But he was not quite convincing.

I swung one leg over the backseat of the little motorcycle taxi, then wobbled from side to side as I tried to balance myself with my luggage. There was no way to hang on. "Take it easy," I pleaded. For once, miraculously, a taxi driver actually did take it easy as we weaved our way around the potholes and bumped down the little dirt road into town. He dropped me off at the town square. Here I was in the pueblo of Santa Ana in northern Bolivia.

With the main highway under several feet of water, it strangely looked much more like a river than a road. Most of the year there are only two ways to get into Santa Ana. You could paddle a canoe for several days, or negotiate airfare with a local pilot and soar over the flooded jungle roads in a private plane. I chose the latter, even at the risk of being mistaken for a drug enforcement agent. The 100 Bolivianos (about U.S. $25) seemed like a steal compared to the canoe ride.

The perpetual buzz of motorcycles around the

town square left little clouds of dust billowing up from their tires. Dogs roamed the streets, unhindered by any fear of leash laws. Schoolchildren with variant-colored backpacks had time for a street game or two as they headed home for the afternoon. All were Santa Ana's ways of greeting a newcomer.

Far we were from the big cities of Bolivia. No foreign travel agent would ever pull out an attractive brochure encouraging "three days and two nights" in this place. Non-Bolivian faces were rare this far up in the Amazon jungles. There was little reason for anyone to come to Santa Ana, tourist or otherwise. I came because a small nucleus of Christians wanted to explore the possibilities of starting a Church of the Nazarene.

"Señor, excuse me. Could you help me, please?" I began to ask directions to Enrique and Delicia's house. No street signs, no house numbers, no city maps, no phones. How could one find the way? The Bolivian system is as simple and effective as it is timeless. Helpful, polite, but often reserved, townsfolk guided me down this and that street and around another corner until at last I found my way to their home.

The Bolivians know how to do coffee right, believe me.

I slipped the suitcase strap off my tired shoulder and set my bags down. I peered through the window of the store that shared a wall with the house. The door was locked tight, and it was dark inside. I stepped to the patio and called their names.

"Hermano Randy," they greeted me happily.

"Come in!" They showed me to the guestroom. With relaxed country work schedules, there was plenty of time to listen to the details of the trip, make our plans for the time I was to be there, and then go to meet some of the other contact families.

The next morning found us on the patio savoring the smell of freshly-baked *pancitos* (small bread rolls), mixed with the irresistible aroma of strong, rich coffee. The Bolivians know how to do coffee right, believe me. There was always a can of Muki brand instant chocolate sitting on the table as well. Just a spoonful or two with the coffee made a great homemade mocha to wash down Delicia's scrumptious pancitos.

The next few days were filled with visits, lively conversations, and a steep learning curve regarding the lives of these folks and the community of Santa Ana. During the long, sultry evenings, we would sit around the small, wooden patio table, lingering far into the night to talk. Myriads of insects accompanied us, seemingly desperate to reach the light as they circled the single bulb that swung from a strand of wire.

Captivating conversations over the Word of God often took us into all the basics of the Christian faith. What does it mean to be a true believer? What about the other churches and religious groups in town? How could we best go about planting this new church? Whatever else happened, be assured that we did our best to encourage a little band of believers and to ask the Lord of the harvest to send them a pastor.

One evening as we sat and talked, Delicia's two younger brothers came for Bible study. In the course of the visit, they told me of their conversion and desire to serve the Lord. One of the brothers, Dennis, also spoke of his call to the ministry. As we prayed together, I felt led of the Lord to make Dennis a promise.

"If you will come to Santa Cruz," I told him, "then I will see to it that you have a place to stay and an opportunity to study in our pastoral training program." Santa Cruz was far, far away, and even an 18-hour bus ride over unpaved roads was expensive enough, not to mention plane tickets. Who could know what might ever come of the offer? I wasn't even sure how I could keep my commitment. All the same, the offer stood.

Long after that conversation entered my mental files of forgetfulness, a Work and Witness team was coming to Bolivia to help build a church in La Paz. One of the preparations was to send them a wooden box full of tools and kitchen supplies. I dutifully hauled the big box to the bus station.

"I want to send this box to La Paz. How much will it cost?"

"Señor, 75 Bolivianos."

"Very well. When will it arrive?"

"In two days."

"Are you sure?"

"Sí, sí," he stated confidently.

I paid the money, and together we lugged the heavy box to the side of the bus.

The Work and Witness team arrived the next

Work and Witness project in Bolivia

week with a brief layover in Santa Cruz. We greeted them briefly and sent them on to La Paz. But the toolbox never arrived, so I went to the bus company to inquire about it. They offered sincere apologies, but the best they could do was to trace it.

The team finished their project, traveled back through Santa Cruz, and returned to the United States. Still not a word about the box.

I made another trip to the bus station to find out what happened.

"Doña, I know it's not your fault," I pleaded with the lady in charge, "but I need to find our toolbox. Our work team has already come, stayed two weeks, finished their work, and gone home again. We still don't have our toolbox. What can you do?" I tried to stay calm.

"We are still trying to trace it. We'll let you know," she offered matter-of-factly.

A couple of days later they called. "We found your toolbox!"

"Where?"

"In Potosí."

"In Potosí?" My ears seemed to be deceiving me. Our toolbox had ended up in a high mountain town far from La Paz.

"I'm very sorry," the agent tried to console me. "We'll send it on to La Paz like you asked."

"Fine, but that doesn't do us much good now," I tried to explain.

I asked to speak to the boss. "Could I get a refund? This shipment has caused us nothing but trouble."

She was adamant. No refunds. "What can you do, then?" I pressed.

"I can have them send the tools back to you here, free of any further charge."

"No, gracias. Please send them on to La Paz."

"Well, here is one thing that I can do," she conceded. "I will give you one free passenger ticket on the bus from Santa Cruz to La Paz. Use it whenever you wish. I'm sorry. That's all I can do."

Neither of us was too happy about the deal. The value of the ticket was considerably less than the shipping costs for the box. I stuck the ticket in my pocket, muttered as polite a "thank you" as I could muster, and left.

Just about a week later, I was absorbed in office work when the phone rang. "Hermano Randy?" a cheery voice sounded in my ears.

"Sí . . . ?" I didn't recognize the person.

"It's Dennis!" he said excitedly. "Can you come pick me up at the bus station?"

My mind was in search mode, trying to think of a way out of the dilemma.

"Sí, sí, of course. In half an hour."

"Hermano Randy, I'm on my way to La Paz to enroll in the seminary," he explained when I picked him up. "All the money I had saved for the trip I spent just to get this far. You promised you would help me . . ." His words hung in the air, the sentence incomplete.

I had promised to help him with the course of study there in Santa Cruz. But if he felt called to go to seminary in La Paz, so much the better. But how to help? My mind was in search mode, trying to think of a way out of the dilemma. I didn't have any spare cash on hand. Then suddenly the scene of the ticket being laid in my hand came to mind.

"Well, I just happen to have a free ticket to La Paz on the bus," I responded. "Let's find out when the next bus leaves, and we'll send you on." I pulled the providential ticket out of my wallet and handed it to him. We talked awhile, then I took him back to the station.

"Gracias, hermano!" He thanked me warmly. We gave each other a firm Bolivian handshake and customary pat on the shoulder, and he stepped onto the bus. He gave me a reassuring final smile through the window as the bus roared out of the station and covered me with diesel smoke.

From that day on, every time I went to La Paz or talked to the seminary director, I wanted to know the latest about Dennis. How were his studies going? Was he doing OK? The answer was always the same:

he was at the top of his class and doing quite well. As Dennis's plans for ministry developed, he wanted to return to his hometown of Santa Ana for evangelism and pastoral ministry.

God had once again reached in with His strong hand and did what He is famous for: working a miracle of grace in the middle of a human situation that seemed difficult—or even impossible. He had grasped hold of a young man's heart and led him into the ministry from a struggling group of believers in a remote village of Bolivia's jungles.

Now are you wondering what I'm wondering? I rather doubt that the Lord purposely delayed a toolbox to provide a bus ticket for a Nazarene seminary student in need. Then again, who am I to say? One thing for sure: God used a human error for His glory. He worked it all together for good for a young man that loved Him and was called according to His purpose.

9
The Visitor

Ana Maria was deaf—to begin with. Yet we had doubts as to how deaf she really was. Certainly she was not stone-deaf, though in my own simple understanding, I'm not sure why a stone is considered any more deaf or cold or blind than any other inanimate object. Indeed, perhaps a Bolivian stone is not quite as deaf as one found in an English-speaking country, for at least a Bolivian stone is seldom referred to as being deaf. If our Lord warned us that the stones might cry out, then how could they be completely deaf anyway? But stones are not our interest here.

"Ana Maria, where do you live?" I asked her the first Sunday she came as a visitor. Her answer was evasive. *Perhaps she doesn't understand me*, I thought. Three shy, stair-step children clung to her as we talked. She had come to visit our church service in Equipetrol. It was a special Sunday evening evangelistic event. Notices had gone throughout the neighborhood, and the building was packed. I'm not sure who gave her an invitation, or if anyone did, but she had heard about the services, and there she appeared with her small children. The ragged clothes they wore sent a message that was loud and clear: they were extremely poor.

Ana Maria did more than visit a first time. She showed up again and again. Whenever she came to church, she seemed to enjoy the service and especially the fellowship. We learned quickly that she could read lips fairly well and could talk enough to get her point across. When we wanted to visit her and get to know her a bit better, we asked once again where she lived. And again we received an evasive answer. Finally, one time I made it clear what I was asking, so she pointed across the road toward the river and said, "We live over there."

There was no more town beyond our Equipetrol church, which was located on the outskirts of Santa Cruz. Just a few hundred feet away, civilization ended and the jungle began, complete with monkeys, mosquitoes, and snakes. The dense brush stretched on quite some distance toward the banks of the Piraí River. That was the direction she had pointed: out in the brush toward the river in an unsettled area. In her "neighborhood," there were no subdivisions, no nice houses, no street numbers, no streets, no streetlights, no telephone lines, no city utilities. No wonder she had been vague; she hardly had a home. Her house was most likely a little lean-to or a makeshift shanty that she and the children had put together with their own hands of branches, cardboard, and tin. The heat and the cold had few impediments to their influence upon her. Possibly a single candle or a simple lantern would be the only heat and light in her one-room dwelling.

She seemed to have only a few family members and limited friends. It is doubtful that anyone would stop her in the marketplace and with smiling face and warm embrace ask, "Ana Maria, when will you come to see me?" She never talked about a husband, and we never pried. She worked odd jobs where her children could be with her all day long. How she kept body and soul together was a mystery.

Ana Maria appeared again at the ladies' Thursday afternoon time of fellowship and handcrafts. All the ladies were so excited when Kathy began to teach them "punto cruz" (cross-stitch). Eagerly learning to turn laborious little stitches into artistic designs, they sat in a circle in the churchyard, talked happily, and laughed when they made a mistake. The group grew until they regularly had 8 to 10 ladies. As the final stitches of the day were added, and the punto cruz cloths were laid aside, they would finish their time with a devotional and prayer. Their souls were fed on the Word, and the practical application to their daily lives led to many a lively discussion of spiritual matters and a time of personal sharing. Ana Maria joined in as well.

Then came the time of our citywide evangelistic campaign. Months of planning and countless hours of intercessory prayer brought all the Nazarene churches in and around Santa Cruz together for those special days of spiritual outpouring. Genuine excitement and effective evangelism characterized the event. One of the keys to its success was the emphasis on united prayer for the unsaved. Lay members had

The ones in charge of the sound turned the volume up to near ear-damaging decibel levels.

agreed to pray for 10 unsaved friends and relatives and then personally invite them to the campaign to hear the gospel. Altogether, several hundred unsaved people were prayed for, and nearly 50 of them came to the services. Each evening new faces next to faithful longtime members filled the benches in the open-air services. What a glorious time we had seeing new people come to hear the Good News and give their hearts to the Lord!

Even the neighbors around the church, whether they came to the services or not, were compelled to hear the music and the messages. Large speakers on the platform towered over the pulpit. The ones in charge of the sound turned the volume up to near ear-damaging decibel levels. They had an interesting rationale: if they turned the volume up loud enough, then the neighbors would have to listen to the service whether they came or not. Even closed shutters could not drown out the sound entirely. There was no community survey to verify how many were impacted by that policy, but the enthusiasm for big speakers and loud volume was hard to contain. I do have a confession to make: somehow, earplugs mysteriously ended up in my pocket on the way to church each evening, and then before the beginning of the service discreetly popped themselves into my ears while no one was looking.

We invited Ana Maria and prayed for her. She came to the services. When asked how she liked the campaign, she smiled, her countenance beaming. "It is such a blessing!" she exclaimed in her halting way. "I'm so glad they turned it up loud enough for me to

Preparing for baptism at Equipetrol church

hear! It was the first time that I have ever been able to understand the whole sermon." We shared a spontaneous, hearty laugh.

She had given a new perspective on that ear-splitting volume. Whoever else in the neighborhood might have heard it, Ana Maria had listened to the gospel message for the first time in its entirety. Before this time, she had heard it in bits and pieces. This time, she had heard the Word of the Lord loudly and clearly and responded with simple faith. For me, just one more picture of grace.

It is to the likes of Ana Maria that Jesus directed His grace and His ministry. She and her children were His business. Her visitation to us was a visitation from the very, very least of these. Jesus said at the beginning of His ministry that "The Spirit of the Lord is upon me, because He anointed me to preach the Gospel to the poor" (Luke 4:18*a*, NASB). No doubt He had Ana Maria in mind. And everyone of us will be blessed as well to minister to all like her.

10
Dieri

Bang, bang, bang! Dieri was knocking on our big iron gate. "¿Está Aarón?" (Is Aaron there?)

Dieri had no other first line. He lived a few blocks down the street from us at the corner of the highway and Calle la Luz. Dieri, a preteen between the age of our sons, Aaron and Arlen, used to walk by the house most every day. It would be somewhat a stretch of the truth to say that we were reaching out to Dieri; it's much more accurate to say that he was reaching out to us.

When things went from casual greeting, to stopping to talk awhile, to his unashamedly asking to come in, we had mixed feelings. We weren't certain what he was after, and we didn't know him well enough to trust him yet. After he came back a time or two, we realized he was harmless and not trying to steal anything. When we invited him in to stay for a while, we didn't have to coax. It quickly became apparent why he was coming: he was starved for affection and friendship—and even for learning.

As the boys accepted him and they became friends, they engaged in animated conversations, teaching him English words and helping him with his schoolwork. If he came at a bad time and we had to say no, he was never discouraged. He was always back later that day or the next.

Although Dieri came to see the boys and they spent time with him, as an observer in the background I found myself drawn to him. Not that I ever disliked him, but I admit that his friendship grew on me over time. He seemed to have just a hint of a learning disability and was so childlike at heart. I began to look forward to seeing him, hearing him talk, ask interesting or even funny questions, and interact with the boys.

Dieri seemed to be one of those people that just imbibed and absorbed the gospel by way of the fellowship of the believers.

One of the most enjoyable things was to see how he looked up to Aaron. No, "looked up to" is hardly an adequate phrase. He did more than look up to Aaron; he fairly idolized him. Aaron was his hero. Our son could do so many things, and, to Dieri, Aaron could do no wrong. Aaron knew how to help him with all his homework. Best of all, along with Arlen, he showed Dieri genuine acceptance and friendship.

"Get in, Dieri, there's room for one more," I assured him one Sunday morning as we all crowded into the taxi to go to church. Bolivian taxis are never big, but then Bolivians aren't worried about riding in a crowded car nor concerned about everyone having a seat belt. Dieri's father had given him permission to attend church with us, and the boy came a number of times whenever he could. He admitted, however, that his papa was not too happy about it.

I don't know where this fits in Wesleyan theology, but Dieri seemed to be one of those people that just imbibed and absorbed the gospel by way of the fellowship of the believers. Though there was no particular day or specific evangelistic service to point to that I am aware of, still he accepted the Kingdom the way the Lord said all of us were to accept it—like a child. God's grace enveloped the lad in a loving embrace.

When we left on home assignment to return to the United States, we were quite uncertain about our future, if we would be reassigned to Santa Cruz or even to Bolivia. At the end of the furlough year, we accepted a new assignment in the Dominican Republic. It fell my lot to return to Bolivia and deal with our stored belongings, shipping them on to the new field. I had one hectic, insane week to sort, sell, pack, and ship everything we owned. While the precious few days I had seemed to evaporate in the tropical sun, I had one important appointment on my to-do list that I could not miss: I had to see Dieri.

When I arrived at his house and walked through the big, shady front yard, he ran to greet me with a hug. It had been over a year since we left, and he was overjoyed to see me. "¿Cómo está Aarón?" (How is Aaron?) was his first line. I expected that to be the first item on his agenda, along with the inevitable question that I dreaded: "When is he coming back?" I fumbled for words as I told him we needed to sit down a minute and talk.

"Here is Aaron's papa," he hollered excitedly to the rest of the family. He ran to bring a couple of chairs.

When I explained that we were being reassigned to the Dominican Republic and that it would be impossible for Aaron and the family to come back to Bolivia, he burst into tears. I slipped my arm around his shoulder, and I confess that his sadness and his sobbing touched me deeply. I gave him a T-shirt and a hat from Aaron. He said he would keep them and treasure them forever.

I could hardly stand to leave. As we said our good-byes, he promised he would read his Bible and would continue to go to church as often as he could. His final teary smile etched itself indelibly into my memory. Dieri will never be forgotten. The Lord reached out to us through a charming Bolivian boy, offering us one more glimpse of God's amazing grace!

Epilogue

The Church of the Nazarene in Bolivia continues to thrive as it reaches new people, plants churches in unchurched neighborhoods, and enters unreached villages with the Good News. Many have talked in recent years about the evangelical revival going on in South America. The holiness message of the Church of the Nazarene is at the heart of that contemporary movement of the Lord. It is bringing an indispensable dimension as the church continues to move ahead and gain strength, looking for the Lord's soon return.

The following statistics for 2004 indicate the excellent growth of the Church of the Nazarene in Bolivia:

- 238 organized churches on 6 districts
- 11,962 church members
- 78 ordained elders and 1 deacon
- 92 licensed ministers
- All 6 districts have superintendents from Bolivia.
- The seminary (Seminario Teológico Nazareno de Bolivia) has a Bolivian director.
- Ed and Lynne Wittung Jr. are the only missionaries.

Here is an update on some of the people you have just learned about in this book:

(L. to r.)
Bolivian pastors: Augusto Suarez (current district superintendent), Oswaldo Soleto, Juan Carlos Vaca and daughter, Macedonio Daza (former district superintendent), and Manuel Suarez

- Dennis is now pastor of the "Manantiales de Vida" (Fountains of Life) church on the Santa Cruz District.
- 27 de Mayo now has a brick sanctuary as well as buildings for a district campground, but awaits the resolution of legal problems on the property.
- Manuel is retired from pastoring, but lives with his children after his wife, Benita, passed away.
- Lucio now pastors the Shaum Memorial Church of the Nazarene in Santa Cruz.
- Rosendo and Gladis are members of the Barrio Lindo church.
- Ignacio, now nearly blind, is in his senior years and lives with his family near the church of Los Junos that he pastored for many years.

Each of the people mentioned in this book has had a part to play in the story of the church in Bolivia. Most of them are not well-known, nor would they want to be. They are out there in that village, just down the road a ways, passing by your gate, perhaps just on the other side of the wall. From well-known leaders, to little-known but faithful local Nazarenes, to new believers just entering the Kingdom, all have been welcomed by God's love and grace into that special group known as "His loved and His own."

"Like the stars of the morning,
His bright crown adorning,
They shall shine in their beauty,
Bright gems for His crown."*

*Refrain of the hymn "Jewels" by William O. Cushing

Call to Action

In response to the information in this book, would you consider doing one or more of the following?

1. Pray for the work of the Church of the Nazarene in Bolivia and for the district superintendents as they provide leadership for the 238 churches.

2. Pray for the president, staff, and students of the Seminario Teológico Nazareno de Bolivia.

3. Pray for missionaries Ed and Lynne Wittung Jr. as they give direction to the work in Bolivia.

4. Pray for Randy Bynum and his family and their ministry to Hispanics in Idaho.

5. Send a card, note, or letter of encouragement to the Wittungs. Their mailing address is Casilla 1757, Cochabamba, Bolivia.

6. Send a card, note, or letter to the Bynums. Their mailing address is 431 Arrowhead Drive, Nampa, ID 83651.

7. Plan a Work & Witness trip to Bolivia. Contact missionary Ed Wittung Jr. about possible locations. Also, you may contact former missionary, Larry Webb, who plans regular Work & Witness trips to Bolivia. The Mavericks, as Larry calls them, are people of all ages from various churches. His address is 6355 Oak Ave. #10, Temple City, CA 91780.

—Wes Eby, editor

Pronunciation Guide

The following information will assist in pronouncing unfamiliar words in this book. The suggested pronunciations, though not always precise, are close approximations of the ways the terms are pronounced. Since these terms are Spanish, the *r* is rolled or trilled in most words.

Ana Maria	AH-nuh mah-REE-ah
Aymara	ie-MAH-rah
Barrio Lindo	BAR-ree-oh LEEN-doh
Bolivianos	boh-LEE-vee-AH-nohs
Buenos días	BWAY-nohs DEE-ahs
Calle la Luz	KAH-yay lah LOOS
campesino	kahm-pay-SEE-noh
centavo	sehn-TAH-voh
chica	CHEE-kah
Cómo está	KOH-moh eh-STAH
Delicia	day-LEE-cee-ah
Dieri	dee-EHR-ee
doña	DOHN-yah
empanadas	ehm-pah-NAH-dahs
Enrique	ehn-REE-kay
Equipetrol	eh-kee-pay-TROHL
Está Aarón	eh-STAH ah-ROHN
Este es el camino	EHS-tay ehs ehl kah-MEE-noh
Gabriel	gah-bree-AYL

Gladis	GLA-dees
Gracia y Devoción	GRAH-see-ah ee day-voh-see-OHN
gracias	GRAH-see-ahs
Gregorio	gray-GOH-ree-oh
hasta luego	HAH-stah loo-AY-goh
hermano	ayr-MAHN-noh
hora Boliviana	OHR-ah boh-LEE-vee-AH-nah
Huarina	wahr-EE-nah
Iglesia del Nazareno	ee-GLAY-see-ah dehl nah-sah-RAY-noh
Ignacio	eeg-NAH-see-oh
intensivo	een-tehn-SEE-voh
Jefe	HEH-fay
Justa	HOO-stah
ladrillos	lah-DREE-yohs
La Paz	lah PAHS
línea dos	LEE-nay-ah DOHS
Llegó el misionero	yay-GOH ehl mee-see-oh-NEHR-oh
Lomas de Arena	LOH-mahs day ah-RAY-nah
Los Junos	lohs HOO-nohs
Lucio	LOO-see-oh
Macedonio Daza	mah-say-DOH-nee-oh DAH-sah
Manantiales de Vida	MAHN-ahn-tee-AH-lays day VEE-dah
Manuel	mahn-WEHL
Marcos	MAHR-kohs
mezcla	MEHS-klah
motacú	moh-tah-KOO
Muki	MOO-kee
pancitos	pahn-SEE-tohs
Paurito	pou-REE-toh
pesos	PAY-sohs

Piraí	pee-rah-EE
Plan Tres Mil	PLAHN TRAYS MEEL
Potosí	poh-toh-SEE
punto cruz	POON-toh KROOS
Que Dios les bendiga ricamente	
	kay DEE-ohs lays
	behn-DEE-gah
	ree-kay-MEHN-TAY
Robertina	roh-behr-TEE-nah
Rosendo	roh-SEHN-doh
Santa Biblia	SAHN-tah BEE-blee-ah
Santa Cruz	SAHN-tah KROOS
Santa Ana	SAHN-tah AH-nah
Seminario Teológico Nazareno de Bolivia	
	say-mee-NAH-ree-oh
	tay-oh-LOH-hee-koh
	nas-ah-RAY-noh day
	boh-LEE-vee-ah
señor	SEHN-yohr
señora	sehn-YOHR-ah
sí	SEE
Titicaca	tee-tee-KAH-kah
uno, dos, y tres	OO-noh DOHS ee TRAYS
Villa Pillín	VEE-yah pee-YEEN
27 de Mayo	vayn-tee-see-EH-tee day
	MAH-yoh